Pumpkins

Joni

Preschool/Kindergarten

Save time and energy planning thematic units with this comprehensive resource. We've searched the 1990–1998 issues of **The MAILBOX®** and **Teacher's Helper®** magazines to find the best ideas for you to use when teaching a thematic unit about pumpkins. Included in this book are favorite units from the magazines, single ideas to extend a unit, and a variety of reproducible activities. Pick and choose from this patch of activities to develop your own complete unit or to simply enhance your current lesson plans. You're sure to find everything you need right here in this book to plant the seeds of learning!

Editors:
Angie Kutzer
Michele M. Menzel

Artists:
Kimberly Richard
Donna K. Teal

Cover Artist:
Cathy Spangler Bruce

www.themailbox.com

Manufactured in the United States
10 9 8 7 6 5 4

Table Of Contents

Thematic Units

Reproducible Activities

Thematic Units...

from **The MAILBOX®** magazine

Pumpkins, Squash, & Gourds

A bale of straw; some produce baskets; and a few dozen pumpkins, squash, and gourds can transform a corner of your preschool classroom into a bustling ever-changing farmers' market.

ideas contributed by Audrey Englehardt and Ruth Stanfill

Getting The Goods

Dig into this theme by starting out in a farmer's pumpkin, squash, or gourd patch. Encourage youngsters (with the farmer's permission, of course) to run their hands along the vines that nurtured their favorite vegetables and analyze the withered leaves that once shaded the immature vegetables. Have students examine and compare twisted lengths of vines. Best of all have them pull a few dozen pumpkins, squash, and/or gourds from the vines to bring back to their classroom.

Down On The Classroom Farm

Once you've returned from your trip to the farm (or otherwise collected a few baskets of pumpkins, squash, and gourds), help your youngsters set up a farmers' market in one corner of the classroom. To add to the market atmosphere, heap the produce in a wheelbarrow and place a bale or two of straw nearby. Label three produce baskets "pumpkins," "squash," and "gourds" respectively; then on each basket attach a picture of the corresponding vegetable. Place the baskets near the produce.

Discuss with students the fact that pumpkins, squash, and gourds are all in the same vegetable family. Explain that just as people in a human family have some characteristics that are similar and some that are different, the vegetables in your classroom market are alike in some ways and different in other ways. If desired, cut open one vegetable of each variety so that students can examine the interiors. After studying the vegetables using their senses of sight, smell, hearing, and touch, guide students in naming several similarities and several differences. Then give youngsters opportunities to sort the contents of the wheelbarrow into the three baskets by vegetable type.

Taking Produce Seriously

Invite your youngsters to man the farmers' market. Encourage volunteer produce peddlers to sort the vegetables into separate piles or baskets by type. Then ask them to line up each type of vegetable on a tabletop from largest to smallest. On another day ask students to line up each type of vegetable on a tabletop from lightest to darkest in color.

A Time To Weigh

Marketing such fine produce can be a weighty matter. Place a set of balance scales in your classroom farmers' market. Give students opportunities to explore the way that the balance scale works. Lead the discussion so that the children discover that the heavier tray of the scale will descend. Then encourage children to visit the center and select pairs of vegetables to compare. Before a child places a vegetable in each side of the balance scale, ask which of the two vegetables he believes will weigh the most. Then have him use the scales to determine which of the two selected

vegetables are actually heavier. Were the results what he expected, or was he surprised? Encourage lots of comparative exploration with the vegetables and the scale.

As students become increasingly comfortable in using the balance scale, have them use it to help answer more complex questions. For example, if one small pumpkin is placed on one side of the scale, how many squash would it take to weigh about the same as the pumpkin? Discuss the fact that when the trays of the scale are at even heights, the trays are holding similar weights.

Great Girth Estimates

What can your students do with string and the largest pumpkin in your collection? Practice estimating skills, of course! Attach three pieces of double-sided tape to a wall near the pumpkin. Label the tape sections "too short," "just right," and "too long." Cut a string length equal to the circumference of your pumpkin. Attach this string to the tape labeled "just right." Have each student cut a length of string to approximate the girth of the pumpkin. Then have him wrap his string around the pumpkin to see how close he was to the actual measurement. Is his string too short, just right, or too long? Have him attach his string to the tape in the appropriate category.

Zucchini
The Great Green Squash

Even those youngsters who think they don't like squash will be easily won over by these muffins. Have students help you in cleaning and shredding the zucchini, as well as in measuring and mixing the remaining ingredients.

Zucchini Muffins

2 cups shredded zucchini
3 eggs
2 cups sugar
3 cups flour
3 teaspoons salt

1/2 teaspoon baking powder
1 teaspoon baking soda
3 teaspoons cinnamon
1 cup oil

Combine the ingredients and beat well. Pour into greased muffin tins or cups. Bake at 375° for approximately 45 minutes, checking for doneness frequently. Makes 24 muffins.

Harvesttime
Centerpieces

Pumpkins, gourds, and squash make beautiful centerpieces. With a nail, poke several holes in a small pumpkin, squash, or gourd for each student. Allow each youngster to select the vegetable he would like to use to create a centerpiece. Have students collect greenery, leaves, and other natural items, then insert the selected items into the holes.

Getting A Feel
For Vegetables

Challenge a small group of children with this fun guessing game. Place a few small pumpkins, gourds, and squash with significantly different shapes and textures in front of a small group of students. Blindfold a volunteer from the group; then pass her one of the vegetables. After giving her an opportunity to thoroughly investigate the vegetable using only her sense of touch, replace the vegetable in its original spot in your collection of vegetables. Then remove the volunteer's blindfold and ask her to identify the pumpkin, gourd, or squash that she examined with her sense of touch. When she identifies the vegetable that she felt, find out how she knows. Then ask for another volunteer to play the game.

Vine Times

On a blacktop or concrete playground surface, use sidewalk chalk to draw a simple network of imitation pumpkin, squash, or gourd vines. Draw a few leaves on the vines. Randomly position three children on the vine design. Ask them to walk heel-to-toe without getting off of the vine. When youngsters arrive at intersections simultaneously, encourage them to cooperate to get around one another without getting off the vine. After each student has had his turn walking on the vine, ask him to use chalk to draw a pumpkin, a squash, or a gourd growing on the vine.

Surprisingly Delicious

Rarely do youngsters get opportunities to sample pumpkin that hasn't been baked into a pie. So this recipe, which uses a pumpkin as an edible baking dish, will be quite an unusual treat!

Pumpkin-Apple Bake

1 small pumpkin
  suitable for baking
chopped apples
raisins

cranberries (optional)
sugar
cinnamon
butter

Preheat oven to 350°. Cut off the top of the pumpkin and scoop out the seeds. Mix chopped apples, raisins, cranberries, sugar, and cinnamon. Pour the mixture into the pumpkin and dot it with butter. Replace the top of the pumpkin. Bake it on a cookie sheet for one hour and 15 minutes to one hour and 30 minutes.

When the pumpkin has sufficiently cooled, scoop out some pumpkin with each serving of apple mixture. Although the pumpkin will darken slightly as it bakes, it will look great as a centerpiece surrounded by smaller pumpkins, squash, gourds, and brightly colored leaves.

Books That Really Grow On Kids

Finding books with just the right amount of text for preschoolers isn't always easy. Both Jeanne Titherington's *Pumpkin Pumpkin* (Greenwillow Books) and Zoe Hall's *It's Pumpkin Time!* (The Blue Sky Press) would complement this pumpkin, squash, and gourd unit. See pages 8 and 9 for a bumper crop of good ideas to use with *Pumpkin Pumpkin*.

Pumpkin Pumpkin

Written & Illustrated by Jeanne Titherington
Published by Greenwillow Books

If autumn seems like one giant "Pumpkin-fest" to you, then make sure you've got several copies of Jeanne Titherington's *Pumpkin Pumpkin* on hand. Soft, detailed illustrations bring the reader right into the garden for a boy's-eye view of the life cycle of a pumpkin plant. From this vantage point, your preschoolers can delight in and learn about the wonders of nature. *Pumpkin Pumpkin* is available in hardcover and paperback.

Pumpkin Pumpkin
by Jeanne Titherington

Cover of *Pumpkin Pumpkin* by Jeanne Titherington. ©1986 by Jeanne Titherington. By permission of Greenwillow Books, a division of William Morrow & Company, Inc.

Setting The Stage

Before students begin to arrive, put a few pumpkin seeds on one tabletop and a pumpkin on another. Invert a cardboard box on the tabletop to cover and hide the seeds, and use another box to hide the pumpkin. In preparation for reading aloud *Pumpkin Pumpkin*, give students opportunities to guess what's covered by each box. Lift the box covering the pumpkin seeds. Being careful to reveal neither that they are seeds nor what kind of seeds they are, have students speculate about what the seeds are. Once it has been determined that the objects are seeds, find out what students think will grow from the seeds. Ask students what seeds need to grow. Find out, for example, if students think the seeds would begin to grow if they were left on a windowsill. Then read aloud *Pumpkin Pumpkin*. Afterward have a student lift the remaining box to see if youngsters' predictions about its contents were right. Encourage students to give a step-by-step description of how the seed was transformed into a pumpkin.

Rolling Along

That was some pumpkin that Jamie grew! Show students the picture in the book of Jamie hauling his pumpkin in a wagon. Find out why your preschoolers think that the wagon was used. In turn, have each child experiment with the best ways to move three pumpkins that vary in weight from very light to heavy. Ask that the child move each pumpkin in three different ways to find out which way is best for moving that particular pumpkin. The first time, have him carry the pumpkin in his arms. The second time, have him put the pumpkin in a box and push or pull it. And finally have him put the pumpkin in a wagon and pull it. When each child has had a chance to experiment with moving the pumpkins, talk about which pumpkins were easiest to carry and which were easiest to haul. Find out what your students think there is about a wagon that helps minimize the effort needed to move a really big pumpkin.

Audrey Englehardt & Ruth Stanfill

Pick Of The Crop

If you're looking for blue-ribbon pumpkin books to use along with *Pumpkin Pumpkin*, look no further.

It's Pumpkin Time!, Written by Zoe Hall, Illustrated by Shari Halpern, Published by Scholastic Inc.

The Pumpkin Patch, Story & Photographs by Elizabeth King, Published by Dutton Children's Books

Pride Of The Patches

Visiting a local farm for a look at a real pumpkin patch is a great way to follow up a reading of *Pumpkin Pumpkin*. While at a farm, students can examine the sizes, textures, and colors of pumpkin plants and pumpkins. And, hopefully, they can see pumpkins in varying stages of development. If there are no pumpkin patches nearby, take youngsters to a produce stand or market. Photograph students with pumpkins of varying sizes—especially some really large ones. (Be sure to make a few pumpkin purchases too. If possible purchase pumpkins in a variety of sizes for later use.) When your photos are developed, have students compare the sizes of the pumpkins they saw with the size of Jamie's pumpkin in *Pumpkin Pumpkin*. Is Jamie's pumpkin larger or smaller than the biggest one they saw? How do they know?

Audrey Englehardt & Ruth Stanfill
South Roxana Elementary
Roxana, IL

Seedy Situation

If you're preparing for autumn, you'll no doubt have your youngsters scraping the seeds from a pumpkin. Have students wash the pumpkin seeds and dump them on several layers of paper towels to dry. Reread the last page of *Pumpkin Pumpkin*. Ask your preschoolers how many seeds Jamie kept for planting next spring. Give each student an opportunity to count out six seeds and put them in an envelope to take home. So that he will remember what the seeds produce, have him draw a pumpkin on the envelope. Plant a few seeds in a large container in the classroom. Encourage students to tend the seeds and comment on what happens.

Wonders Never Cease
Simple Science For Young Children

Pumpkin Patch Science

Here's a pumpkin patch filled with activities using one of autumn's favorite foods. Gather an assortment of small, medium, and large pumpkins; then use the ideas in this unit to get your youngsters into pumpkin science!

ideas by Dr. Suzanne Moore

Objective: Students will learn that a pumpkin comes from a plant, and that both the inside and the seeds can be eaten.

It's Pumpkin Time

Set the scene for your study of pumpkins by reading *It's Pumpkin Time!* by Zoe Hall (The Blue Sky Press). Bold illustrations introduce the life cycle of the pumpkin from seed to harvest.

Our Pumpkin—Outside

Orange
Rough
Lumpy
Big
We can make a pumpkin pie!

27"

15 pounds

Our Pumpkin—Inside

Pumpkin Properties

In this activity, students will use their senses and oral language to observe and communicate about pumpkins.

For each small group, you will need:

a pumpkin   measuring tape
markers   large chart paper
a scale

Begin by gathering a small group of children around the pumpkin. Ask questions to prompt your young scientists to look at, touch, smell, weigh, and measure the pumpkin. Encourage them to comment on what they discover about the pumpkin. Write children's responses on a large sheet of chart paper titled "Our Pumpkin" (see the illustration). Save the chart to use later!

Did You Know...

Although most pumpkins are various shades of orange, some varieties are white, yellow, or even other colors.

Our Pumpkin—Inside

Youngsters will harvest a pumpkin patch full of science when they gather more data about the inside of your class pumpkins.

For each small group, you will need:

a scale   a large spoon
a sharp knife   a bowl
the pumpkin chart from "Pumpkin Properties"
newspaper (or similar) for table covering

In turn, gather each small group and review its pumpkin property chart. Ask how they think the inside of the pumpkin might look. After discussing ideas, cut off the top of the pumpkin. Encourage students to peek inside and use their senses to explore the inside of the pumpkin. Record student observations on the chart. Next scoop the seeds and pulp into the bowl. Then have the group weigh its pumpkin and compare the new weight to its original weight.

Our Pumpkin—Outside
Orange
Rough
Lumpy
Big
We can make a pumpkin pie!
← 27" →
15 pounds

Our Pumpkin—Inside
It smells good!
It looks yucky.
After we took out the seeds it weighed...
13 pounds

Did You Know...

Since the early 1800s, prizes have been awarded for the heaviest pumpkins at regional fairs. One winning pumpkin at the World Pumpkin Confederation tipped the scales at 1,061 pounds!

Clean...

Distribute a paper plate and a portion of the seeds and stringy fiber to each child in the group. Give him a magnifying glass, inviting him to carefully explore the contents. Then ask each child to separate the seeds from the fiber. Collect the seeds and let them dry in single layers on paper plates or a tray. Save the seeds for further activities.

...And Count

When the seeds are dry, encourage youngsters to examine them again. Do the seeds look different? How? Then have the class work together to count all of the seeds—perhaps your class would like to count by fives, or tens? Record the number of seeds on each chart. Then have each child glue a few dried seeds around the edges of his group's chart. Maybe your youngsters would even like to taste a few!

Our Pumpkin—Outside
Orange
Rough
Lumpy
Big
We can make a pumpkin pie!
← 27" →
15 pounds

It smells good!
It looks yucky.
After we took out the seeds it weighed...
13 pounds

We Know Pumpkins, Outside And In!

This activity will not only reinforce the fact that pumpkins grow on vines, but will also create an eye-catching display. Duplicate a class supply of page 15 on construction paper. Have each child sponge-paint and cut out his pumpkins. When the paint is dry, ask each child to write his name on the outside and add crayon details as desired. Then have him glue orange yarn fibers and real seeds to the inside pattern. Staple the outside pumpkin to the inside pumpkin along the left edge. Then mount each pumpkin on a white bulletin-board background. Add green crepe-paper vines. For leaves, have each child trace his hands on green construction paper, then cut out the shapes. Add a title, and you're set—outside and in!

The Pumpkin Float

Will pumpkins float? Gather small pumpkins, a yes-no class graph, one pumpkin cutout for each child, plastic tubs, and water; then find out! Begin by asking your students if they think a pumpkin will float in water. Have them indicate their responses by taping their pumpkin cutouts in the appropriate column of the graph. Then fill the plastic containers with enough water so that each pumpkin will not hit the bottom of the container. Invite children to set the pumpkins in the water. Do they float? Can they imagine why?

Did You Know...

A long time ago, it rained so much and so hard that some pumpkin fields became flooded. Because of all the water, thousands of pumpkins went floating along into the villages!

Check It Out!
Pumpkin Books

Big Pumpkin
Written by Erica Silverman
Illustrated by S. D. Schindler
Published by Macmillan, 1992

The Biggest Pumpkin Ever
Written by Steven Kroll
Illustrated by Jeni Bassett
Published by Holiday House, Inc.; 1984

Grandma's Smile
Written by Elaine Moore
Illustrated by Dan Andreasen
Published by Lothrop, Lee & Shepard
    Books; 1995

The Great Pumpkin Switch
Written by Megan McDonald
Illustrated by Ted Lewin
Published by Orchard Books, 1992

Five Little Pumpkins
Written & Illustrated by
    Iris Van Rynbach
Published by Boyds Mills Press, 1995

Jeb Scarecrow's Pumpkin Patch
Written & Illustrated by Jana Dillon
Published by Houghton Mifflin
    Company, 1992

The Pumpkin Patch
Written & Photographed by
    Elizabeth King
Published by Dutton Children's
    Books, 1990

Pumpkin Pumpkin
Written & Illustrated by Jeanne
    Titherington
Published by Greenwillow Books, 1986

©The Education Center, Inc. • *Pumpkins* • Preschool/Kindergarten • TEC3174

Check It Out!
Pumpkin Books

Big Pumpkin
Written by Erica Silverman
Illustrated by S. D. Schindler
Published by Macmillan, 1992

The Biggest Pumpkin Ever
Written by Steven Kroll
Illustrated by Jeni Bassett
Published by Holiday House, Inc.; 1984

Grandma's Smile
Written by Elaine Moore
Illustrated by Dan Andreasen
Published by Lothrop, Lee & Shepard
    Books; 1995

The Great Pumpkin Switch
Written by Megan McDonald
Illustrated by Ted Lewin
Published by Orchard Books, 1992

Five Little Pumpkins
Written & Illustrated by
    Iris Van Rynbach
Published by Boyds Mills Press, 1995

Jeb Scarecrow's Pumpkin Patch
Written & Illustrated by Jana Dillon
Published by Houghton Mifflin
    Company, 1992

The Pumpkin Patch
Written & Photographed by
    Elizabeth King
Published by Dutton Children's
    Books, 1990

Pumpkin Pumpkin
Written & Illustrated by Jeanne
    Titherington
Published by Greenwillow Books, 1986

©The Education Center, Inc. • *Pumpkins* • Preschool/Kindergarten • TEC3174

I am perfectly pleased to report that ____ can tell you all about pumpkins!

Name ____

I know pumpkins—outside and in! Ask me to tell you about them!

_____
knows pumpkins, outside...

and in!

Parachute Pumpkins

Give parachute play a pumpkin twist. Gather several orange beach balls or foam balls, and pretend that they are pumpkins. Have youngsters gather around a parachute and stretch it taut. Toss the pumpkins onto the parachute, and invite little ones to make them shake and shimmy as you chant the following rhyme. When you reach the last line of the rhyme, encourage little ones to make the pumpkins jump right off the parachute.

Pumpkins round and pumpkins fat;
Jump on the parachute just like that!

Pumpkins high and pumpkins low;
Pumpkins, pumpkins, off you go!

Amy Rain Monahan—Four-Year-Olds
Evangelical School For The Young Years
Godfrey, IL

The Pumpkins Are Here

After introducing the song, give each youngster a pumpkin cutout that has been mounted on a straw or a craft stick. As the song is sung, have each youngster hold his pumpkin as indicated by the words.

(sung to the tune of "The Farmer In The Dell")

The pumpkins are here; the pumpkins are there.
The pumpkins, the pumpkins are everywhere.

The pumpkins are up; the pumpkins are down.
The pumpkins, the pumpkins are all around.

The pumpkins are in; the pumpkins are out.
The pumpkins, the pumpkins are all about.

The pumpkins are low; the pumpkins are high.
The pumpkins, the pumpkins all say, "Good-bye."

Lucia Kemp Henry

Patch Of Ideas ● ● ● ●

Clip the pumpkins to the patch in order.

Clip It!

This file-folder activity can be made to enhance a pumpkin unit and to reinforce numeral sequencing. Draw or attach art to the far left and far right sides of the inside of a file folder. Laminate the folder. Cut a slit for each space that you would like to have in the activity. Slip one side of a paper clip into each of the slits. Secure each paper clip in place by taping the other side of the paper clip to the back of the folder. Write directions on the folder with a permanent marker. Make three reduced copies of the pumpkin cards on page 48. Color, laminate, cut out, and program the seasonal pumpkin cards. Store the cards in a zippered plastic bag. To do this activity, a youngster clips the cards to the folder in numerical order.

Pick A Pumpkin
(sung to the tune of "London Bridge")

Pick a pumpkin from the vine.   *Pretend to pick up a pumpkin.*
Pumpkin round, pumpkin fine.   *Gesture to indicate "big and round."*
Pick a pumpkin from the vine.   *Pretend to pick up a pumpkin.*
Let's pick pumpkins!   *Gesture, "Come with me!"*

Pick a pumpkin from the vine.   *Pretend to pick up a pumpkin.*
You pick yours. I'll pick mine.   *Point to indicate "you" and "me."*
Pick a pumpkin from the vine.   *Pretend to pick up a pumpkin.*
Let's pick pumpkins!   *Gesture, "Come with me!"*

Betty Silkunas, Lansdale, PA

Pumpkin Bread

Have youngsters make these individual pumpkin bread loaves to share with their families. In advance, collect one empty soup can per child, and remove the labels. Mix together all the ingredients for a double-size batch of pumpkin bread. Pour a small amount of the mixture into each soup can. Bake the mixture in the cans. When cooled, your youngsters will have miniature loaves of tasty pumpkin bread to take home. Yum!

Lynn Sanders—Gr. K, Hayes Elementary School, Marietta, GA

Pumpkin Vocabulary

If you have a pumpkin in your classroom, the teachable moment for this activity is bound to pop up. As children examine the pumpkin, encourage them to use descriptive vocabulary to tell about the pumpkin. Write the words on masking tape; then attach them to the pumpkin.

Jane K. Frain—Gr. K
North Harlem Elementary
Harlem, GA

Ribbed Round Hard Fat Cute Orange Big

A Gift To Pass On

If you carve a pumpkin with your class, here's a neat gift idea that your youngsters can pass on to next year's kindergartners. Dry and save several of the pumpkin seeds. In May, plant the seeds. Then your new crop of kindergartners will have pumpkins to harvest in the fall!

Betty L. Gomillion—Gr. K, South Leake Elementary, Walnut Grove, MS

"Pumpkin feels squishy." John

"There are a zillion seeds inside." Tika

Pumpkin Exploration

Encourage students to explore and record their discoveries with this seasonal science activity. Place a pumpkin in a shallow tub in your science center. Cut the top off the pumpkin or cut the pumpkin in half so that little ones can observe and feel the inside as well as the outside of the pumpkin. Provide plastic knives and spoons for the children to use when exploring the pumpkin. Near the center, post a large, pumpkin-shaped chart cut from orange poster board. As children visit the center, record their discoveries on the chart. Be sure to have disposable wipes available for a quick cleanup after students' sticky studies!

Ann Endorf—Preschool
Open Arms Christian Preschool
Bloomington, MN

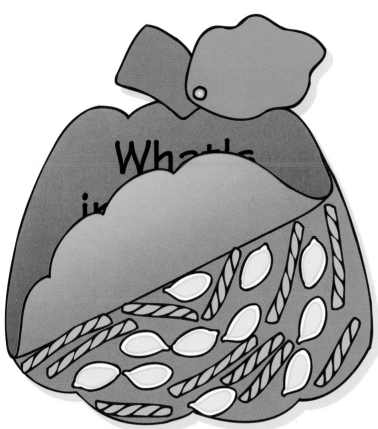

Plenty Of Pumpkin, Plenty Of Seeds!

That's what youngsters will find when you give them the opportunity to dig into a topless pumpkin. It's also what they'll find when they peek into this crafty pumpkin! From construction paper, cut a stem, a leaf, and two identically shaped pumpkins. Title one of the pumpkin cut-outs "What's Inside A Pumpkin?"; then glue on the stem and leaf. To one side of the other pumpkin cutout, glue short pieces of orange yarn and real pumpkin seeds that have been washed and dried. Assemble the shapes with a brad as shown; then take a pumpkin peek!

Sonja M. Harrington—Pre-K
Tiny Tears Day Care
Albemarle, NC

Seasonal Spyglasses

Scope out these terrific spyglasses to help reinforce color-recognition skills. To make a spyglass, cut out two identical shapes from construction paper. Cut out identical portions of the shapes' centers. Tape a matching color of cellophane over the center of one of the shapes; then glue the shapes together. Encourage your little ones to use the spyglasses to look at things in the classroom, then name the colors they see.

Bernadette Hoyer—Four- And Five-Year-Olds
Howard B. Brunner School
Scotch Plains, NJ

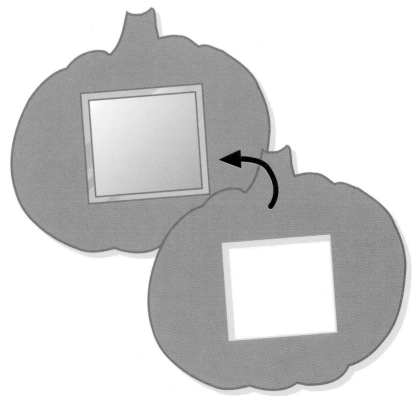

To grow the biggest pumpkin ever...

Try this board as a perfect follow-up to Steven Kroll's *The Biggest Pumpkin Ever* (Cartwheel Books). Draw a giant pumpkin on white bulletin-board paper. Cut the pumpkin into puzzle pieces—one for each child. Ask each child what he would do to grow the biggest pumpkin ever. Record his response on his pumpkin piece. Have each child color his piece before reassembling the entire pumpkin on a board with related cutouts and a title. That is the biggest pumpkin ever!

Brenda Henry—Gr. K, Teutopolis Elementary, Teutopolis, IL

Pumpkin Harvest Fun

Try this special harvesttime activity for a great pumpkin-patch display. In advance, collect a quantity of half-pint milk cartons; then cut the tops off them. Give each student one milk carton. To decorate it, have him glue orange construction paper to the outside of it. Then have him half-fill his carton with potting soil. As students look on, cut the top off a large pumpkin. Allow each child to take a couple of seeds out of the pumpkin, then rinse the seeds with water. Have him plant his pumpkin seeds in the soil. Clean the rest of the pumpkin; then set it aside for later use. Next cover a table with brown paper, and have each child place his milk carton atop the paper. Encourage your youngsters to paint vines and leaves on the paper connecting one milk-carton pumpkin to another. Place the pumpkin on the table to complete the pumpkin-patch display. Water the pumpkin seeds as necessary to keep the soil moist. Encourage youngsters to watch their pumpkin patch grow!

Anne Leach—Gr. K, St. Ann's, Charlotte, NC

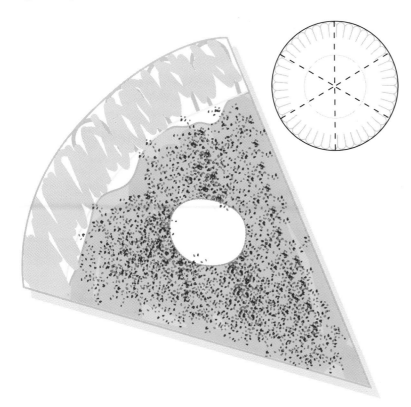

A Slice Of Spice!

Spice up your room with this project that's "scent-sational." In advance, cut several paper plates into sixths to resemble pie slices. To make a slice of pumpkin pie, color the outside rim of a slice brown to resemble the crust. Paint the remaining portion orange to resemble the pumpkin filling. While the paint is still wet, sprinkle it with pumpkin-pie spices such as ground cinnamon, ginger, or cloves. Glue a cotton ball on the pie slice to resemble a dab of whipped cream.

Ellyn Jaeger—Preschool, Wee Know Nursery School, Dousman, WI

Pumpkin Pie Song

Encourage youngsters to create their own motions for this tasty treat of a song. If a trip to a pumpkin patch is planned, follow up the outing by cooking pumpkin pie. Be sure to take pictures that correspond to each verse of the song; then use the pictures and the text of the song to create a book.

(sung to the tune of "Paw Paw Patch")

Where, oh, where are all the children?
Where, oh, where are all the children?
Where, oh, where are all the children?
Way down yonder in the pumpkin patch!

Pickin' up a pumpkin. Put it in the wagon…

Take it home and cut it open…

Cut it all up. Mash it and mash it…

Pour it in the piecrust. Put it in the oven…

Bake it and bake it until it's ready…

Put it in my tummy. Yummy! Yummy!…

Dr. Grace Morris, Southwest Texas State University
San Marcos, TX

Not even the Great Pumpkin would think of this pumpkin display! Cut out and mount one pumpkin shape and up to three leaves per student. Add lengths of green yarn for vines. Mount student snapshots atop the pumpkin cutouts. Now that's a patch of pride!

Beverly Hargrove Free—Gr. KL, Ridge Elementary, Lafayette, LA

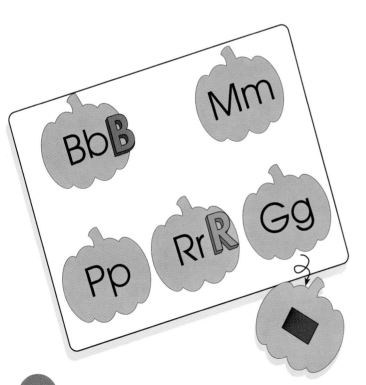

Pumpkin Patch Fun

Reinforce letter recognition with this magnetic center that will attract attention. For each letter that you wish to study, cut out a pumpkin shape from construction paper. Program each pumpkin with an upper-case and matching lowercase letter. Laminate the cutouts if desired; then attach a piece of magnetic tape to the back of each piece. Place the cutouts, an alphabet of magnetic letters, and a magnetic board in a center. To use this center, a child arranges a few pumpkin cut-outs on the magnetic board. Then he matches the magnetic letters to the corresponding pumpkins.

Melissa Iverson
Academy Park Elementary
Bountiful, UT

Pumpkin Tambourine

Celebrate the harvest by shaking a pumpkin tambourine! To make one, paint the backs of two paper plates orange. When the paint is dry, secure the rims of the plates together with several paper clips; then use a hole puncher to punch an even number of holes through the rims. Remove the paper clips. Through every pair of holes, thread a length of green yarn through both plates. Thread a jingle bell onto the yarn; then tie the yarn in a bow. Shake, shake, shake that tambourine!

The Pumpkin Seed Game

Scoop out your class pumpkin and roast the seeds for an exciting class game. Have students sit on the floor in a circle. Place two paper plates in front of each child. Place a handful of roasted pumpkin seeds on one plate for each child. Give each student a plastic drinking straw. Demonstrate how to move the seeds from one plate to the other by sucking them up, one at a time, with the straw. Allow children to practice; then give a signal to start transferring the seeds! The winner is the child who transfers the most pumpkin seeds to his empty plate before the time's up! After the game, everyone gets to snack on the seeds.

Joyce Montag, Slippery Rock, PA

Seasonal Door Decoration

Your youngsters are probably already going to make the ingredients for this eye-catching display—you just need to quilt them all together. Cover a door with butcher paper; then add construction-paper dividers to form squares. Mount a child's autumn craft—such as a pumpkin or an ear of Indian corn—in each of the squares. Using glitter glue, write "Quilting Autumn Treasures" on construction-paper banners. When the lettering is dry, tape the banners across the quilt. Just beautiful!

Rena McCall—Gr. K
Anne Watson Elementary
Bigelow, AR

"I Am Here!"

Take attendance and help little ones practice name recognition with this management aid. Personalize a decorated index card or seasonal cutout for each child. Cut one piece of Velcro® tape for each cutout. Peel the paper off the back of each Velcro® piece. Attach the loop side of each piece to the back of a different card or cutout. On a wall, within your youngsters' reach, mount the hook side of each Velcro® tape piece. Attach the cards or cutouts to the wall. Make a large tagboard pocket and program the front of it with "I am here." Then mount the pocket on the wall. Each morning, as each student enters your room, have him locate his name-tag, remove it from the wall, and place it in the "I Am Here" pocket. With this quick-and-easy method, you can tell at a glance which children are present.

Debbie Brown—Four-Year-Olds
Corson Park Day Care
Millville, NJ

Pokin' Around The Pumpkin Patch!

It's time to go pokin' around the pumpkin patch! Add a brown paper fence to a black background. To fill the patch with pumpkins, have each child stuff a paper lunch-size bag with newspaper, twist the top, and secure it with a rubber band. Have each child paint her bag to resemble a pumpkin. Pin the pumpkins to the board. Add a friendly scarecrow character to the board to guard the patch until the pumpkins are ripe for picking!

Nancy Hayes—Gr. K, Victor Haen School, Kaukauna, WI

Magic Pumpkins

Treat your little ones to a color-mixing lesson inspired by the color of Halloween—orange. On art paper, have each youngster paint a large, red, circular shape. Before the paint begins to dry, have him paint over the red paint with yellow, blending thoroughly. When dry, have students cut out the orange circles and attach green paper stems to create a class pumpkin patch.

Kathleen McCarthy—Gr. K
Frankfurt American Elementary School
Frankfurt, Germany

Put on your apron and step into the kitchen—with your kids, of course! What's on the menu? A generous portion of learning opportunities served up with a batch of fun. Savor the following two hands-on cooking activities perfectly measured for student fun and teacher ease.

Here's what to do:

- Collect the necessary ingredients and utensils using the list on one of the recipe cards below.
- Follow the teacher preparation guidelines for that cooking activity.
- Photocopy, color, and cut out the step-by-step directions on pages 27 and 28.
- Display the step-by-step directions in sequence in your cooking area so that the students can see the directions for the recipe you've selected.
- Discuss the directions with a small group of kids; then encourage them to get cooking!

Learning has never been so delicious!

Pumpkin Shake

Ingredients:
1 can of solid-pack pumpkin
1 pint of skim milk for every 32 children
1/2 gallon of vanilla frozen yogurt
   for every 16 children
1 candy pumpkin per child

Utensils And Supplies:
1 plastic cup per child
1 straw per child
teaspoon
tablespoon
1/2-cup measuring cup

Teacher Preparation:
   Allow the frozen yogurt to soften slightly. Arrange the ingredients and utensils near the step-by-step direction cards on page 27.

Frozen Pumpkin Squares

Ingredients For One:
two square graham crackers
1 tsp. pumpkin-pie filling
3 Tbs. whipped topping

Utensils And Supplies:
tablespoon
teaspoon
bowl
serving spoons
freezer

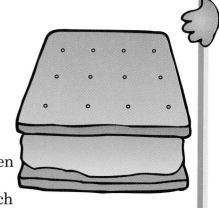

Teacher Preparation:
Have a cookie sheet available to hold the ready-to-be-frozen pumpkin squares. Arrange the ingredients and utensils near the step-by-step direction cards on page 28. Have each cook place his pumpkin square on the sheet.

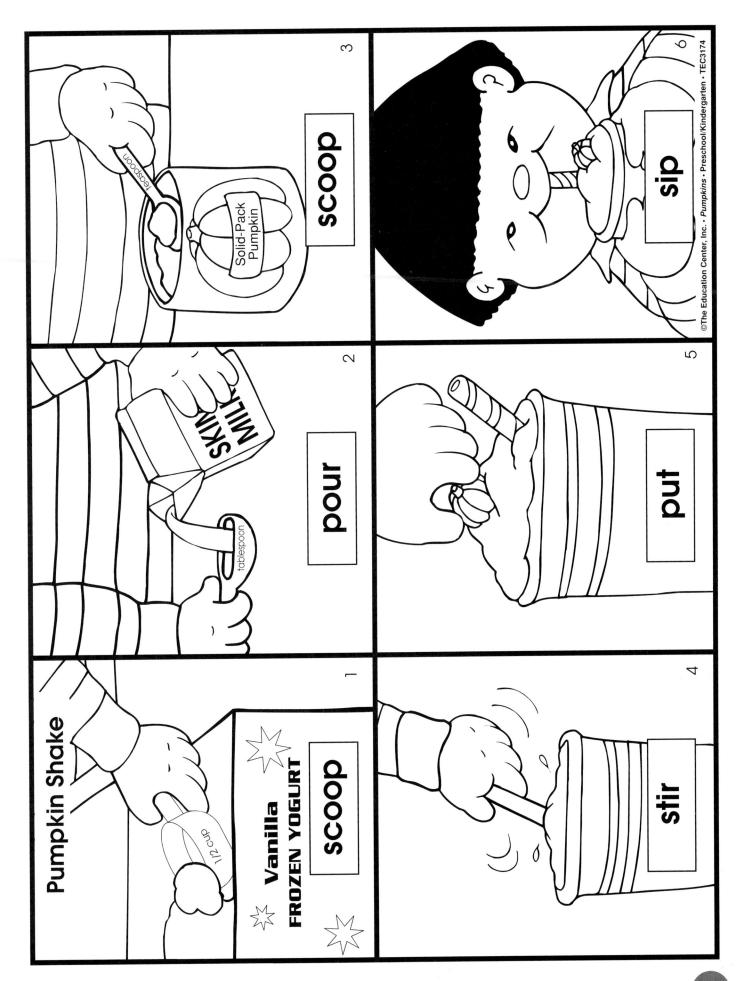

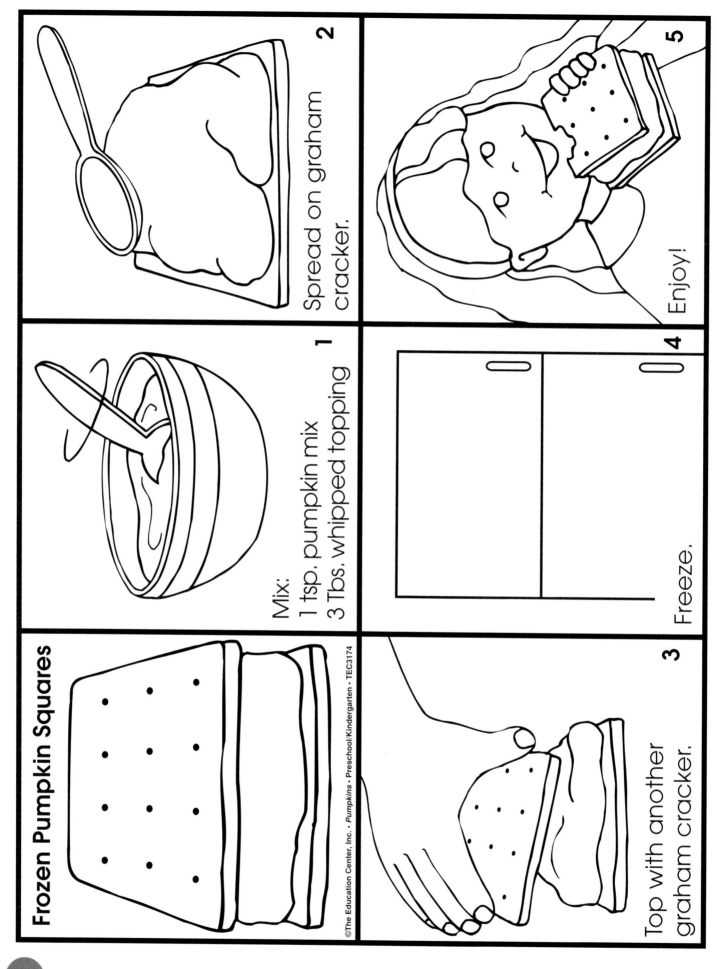

Frozen Pumpkin Squares

1 Mix:
1 tsp. pumpkin mix
3 Tbs. whipped topping

2 Spread on graham cracker.

3 Top with another graham cracker.

4 Freeze.

5 Enjoy!

Signs Of Autumn

What better way to gather up signs of autumn than to head outdoors for an autumn hunt? Provide each child with a resealable plastic bag. Have each of your little ones search for and collect signs of autumn such as pinecones, leaves, nuts, twigs, and acorns. When the hunt is over, return to the classroom. Supply each child with a tagboard pumpkin shape and glue. Have him glue the items from his bag onto his cutout.

W. L. Harris, Columbia, MD

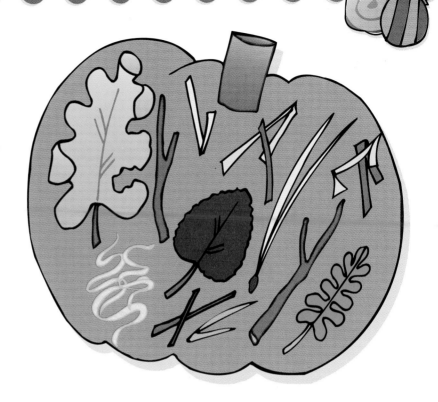

Gather your youngsters to help you make this display. Mount a bulletin-board-paper tree; then adorn it with students' sponge-painted leaf shapes. Have students glue orange and green tissue-paper pieces to paper plates to make a patch of pumpkins; then pile the pumpkins beneath the tree. You're really harvesting now!

Laura Fitz—Pre-K, Baltimore County Public School, Baltimore, MD

Mr. Pumpkin

Mr. Pumpkin had better beware! Harvest-time is coming and that is that!

(sung to the tune of "Frère Jacques")

Mr. Pumpkin,
Mr. Pumpkin,
Round and fat.
Round and fat.
Harvesttime is coming.
Harvesttime is coming.
Yum, yum, yum.
That is that!

Michelle Johnson and René Jenkins
Lakeland, FL

Pumpkin Patch Surprise

Combine a surprise pumpkin patch with a family picnic. Announce the date of a class picnic and pumpkin hunt to parents. Keeping the patch a secret from youngsters, ask parents to donate small pumpkins to your class. Before youngsters arrive at school on the morning of the picnic, arrange the pumpkins in an open area of your school's playground. Enjoy a day of pumpkin picking and picnicking!

adapted from an idea by Linda N. Roth—
    Four- And Five-Year-Olds
First Step Preschool
Black Forest, CO

I Spy Pumpkin Pie

I spy pumpkin pie—and smell pie, too! These crafty pumpkin pies smell just like the real thing. Fill a paper bowl with torn, orange tissue-paper pieces. Spray the pieces with cinnamon-scented air freshener. While the pieces are damp, sprinkle on pumpkin-pie spice. Trace the top of an empty bowl onto a piece of orange paper; then cut out the circle. Punch holes through the circle; then glue the circle onto the rim of the "pumpkin-filled" bowl. Present these air fresheners as gifts, and spicy thank-yous are sure to follow.

adapted from an idea by Charlet Keller—Preschool
ICC Preschool, Violet Hill, AR

Reproducible Activities...

Pumpkin Pumpkin

Cover of *Pumpkin Pumpkin* by Jeanne Titherington. ©1986 by Jeanne Titherington.
By permission of Greenwillow Books, a division of William Morrow & Company, Inc.

Note To The Teacher

This unit has been designed to be used with *Pumpkin Pumpkin* by Jeanne Titherington (Greenwillow Books). This unit is also part of the integrated theme units. The pumpkin-related shapes on page 48 and math units on pages 38–46 will extend the literature unit and will be springboards for additional studies about pumpkins.

How To Use Page 33.

1. Review or read aloud the story *Pumpkin Pumpkin*.
2. Discuss what happened to Jamie and the pumpkin in the story.
3. Call attention to the pictures on page 33. Discuss which pictures show what happened in the story; then have the students color those pictures.

Background For The Teacher
Pumpkins

Pumpkins are round and oval fruits that have hard shells and coarse, stringy pulp. Inside the pumpkin is a central cavity that holds the seeds. Pumpkins are an extremely versatile food source. They can be boiled, baked, and even dried. Cooked and mashed pumpkin can be eaten plain or used in pies, puddings, and breads.

Pumpkins grow in slightly acid soil. After the seeds are planted, most pumpkins grow and mature in about four months. Pumpkin vines take up considerable space in the garden. One plant can cover more than 20 square feet of ground.

Pumpkins range in size from palm-sized to those weighing as much as 200 pounds. Most pumpkins are orange; however, some are white, yellow, or other colors.

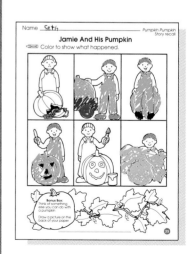

Name

Jamie And His Pumpkin

Color to show what happened.

Bonus Box:
Think of something else you can do with a pumpkin.

Draw a picture on the back of your paper.

How To Use Page 35

If desired, again read aloud *Pumpkin Pumpkin* before having each student complete this activity. Talk with youngsters about what they think pumpkins need in order to grow. Then read and discuss each of the following statements, and direct students as indicated in italics.

1. Pumpkins need soil to grow. We plant pumpkin seeds in soil. The roots grow in the soil. *Color the soil brown.*
2. Pumpkins need water to grow. Sometimes rain falls on the pumpkin plant, and sometimes we water the pumpkin plant. *Draw and color blue water coming out of the watering can.*
3. Pumpkins need sun to grow. The sun helps the leaves make food for the pumpkin plant. *Draw and color a yellow sun in the sky.*
4. *Finish the picture by coloring the leaves green and the pumpkin orange.*

How To Use This Page

1. Duplicate the award pattern on this page for each child.
2. After students complete the "Growing Pumpkins" worksheet (page 35), have each of them color, cut out, fold, and glue an award pattern. Then have each child write his name in the space provided.
3. Drop a handful of clean, dry pumpkin seeds into the envelope pocket.

Award

Pumpkin Seeds

_____
name

has worked hard to learn how pumpkins grow.

Try growing pumpkins next spring!

©The Education Center, Inc.

fold

fold

fold

Glue here.

Glue here.

Growing Pumpkins

What do pumpkins need to grow?
Listen and do.
 Color.

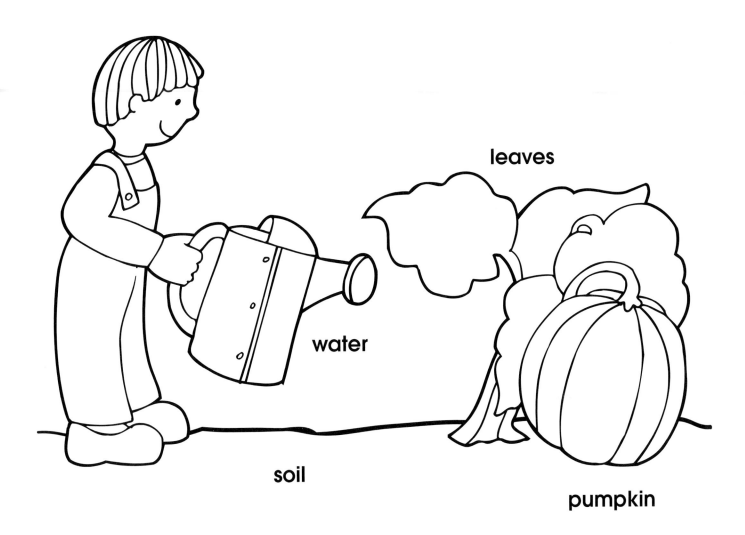

sun

leaves

water

soil

pumpkin

Pumpkins need soil.

Pumpkins need water.

Pumpkins need sun.

How To Use Pages 36 And 37

1. For each child, duplicate pages 36 and 37.
2. Have each child color the cover and each of the six booklet pages, then cut on the bold lines.
3. Stack the pages in the correct order and staple them together.
4. Read the booklet aloud with your youngsters.

"Pumpkins Grow" Booklet

Read.

 Color.

Cut.

Staple.

Pumpkins Grow

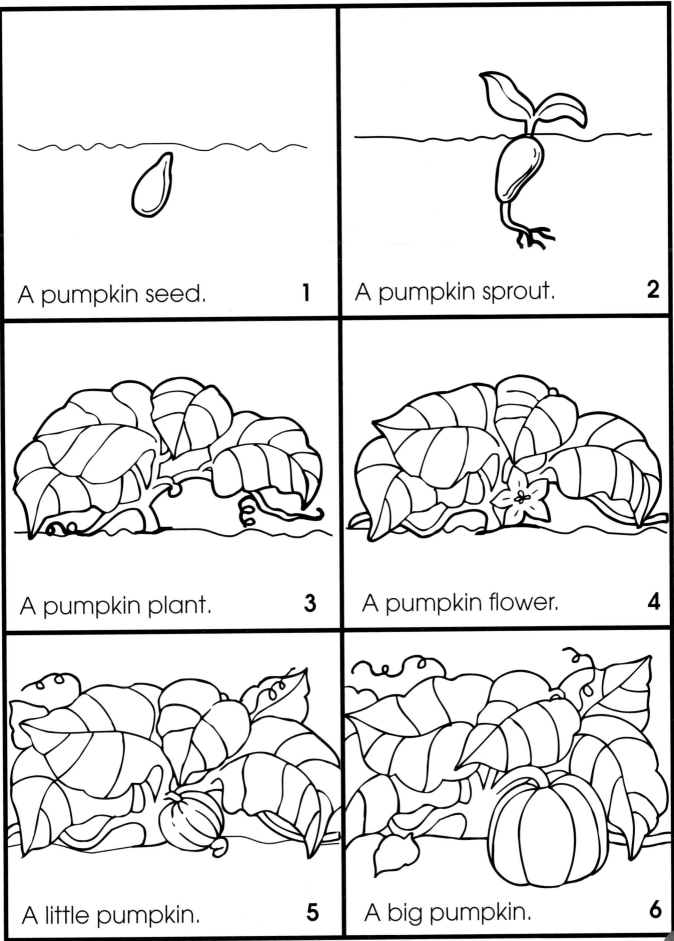

A pumpkin seed.　　1

A pumpkin sprout.　　2

A pumpkin plant.　　3

A pumpkin flower.　　4

A little pumpkin.　　5

A big pumpkin.　　6

Pumpkins & Pumpkin Seeds

Materials Needed

—miniature pumpkins
  (one for each small group of students)
—crayons
—knife

—art paper
—glue

How To Use Page 39

1. In advance, collect miniature pumpkins (roughly baseball size) for this reporting activity.
2. Duplicate the page for each child.
3. Divide students into small groups and assign each group a pumpkin.
4. To complete the page, have each student draw and color his group's pumpkin in the space with the pumpkin sketch.
5. Beside his pumpkin picture, have each child indicate the size of his group's pumpkin by coloring.
6. Cut open each group's pumpkin; then assist students in separating the seeds from the pulp. Arrange the seeds on sheets of art paper. Have each student estimate how many seeds there are, then write his guess in the space provided.
7. Next count the seeds to determine the total number. Have each student write the number of seeds found in his group's pumpkin.
8. When the seeds have dried, have each youngster glue a few in the space provided.

Finished Sample

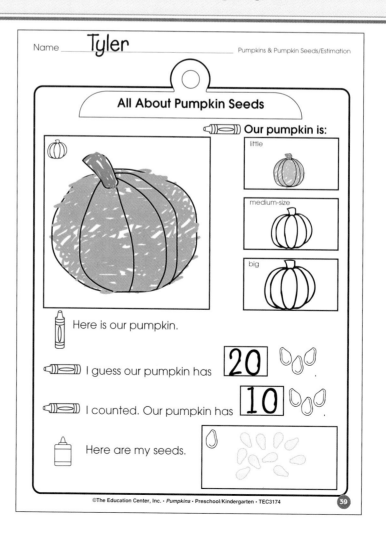

All About Pumpkin Seeds

 Our pumpkin is:

little

medium-size

big

 Here is our pumpkin.

 I guess our pumpkin has   .

 I counted. Our pumpkin has  .

 Here are my seeds.

Name _____

Pumpkin Patch Counting

Count. 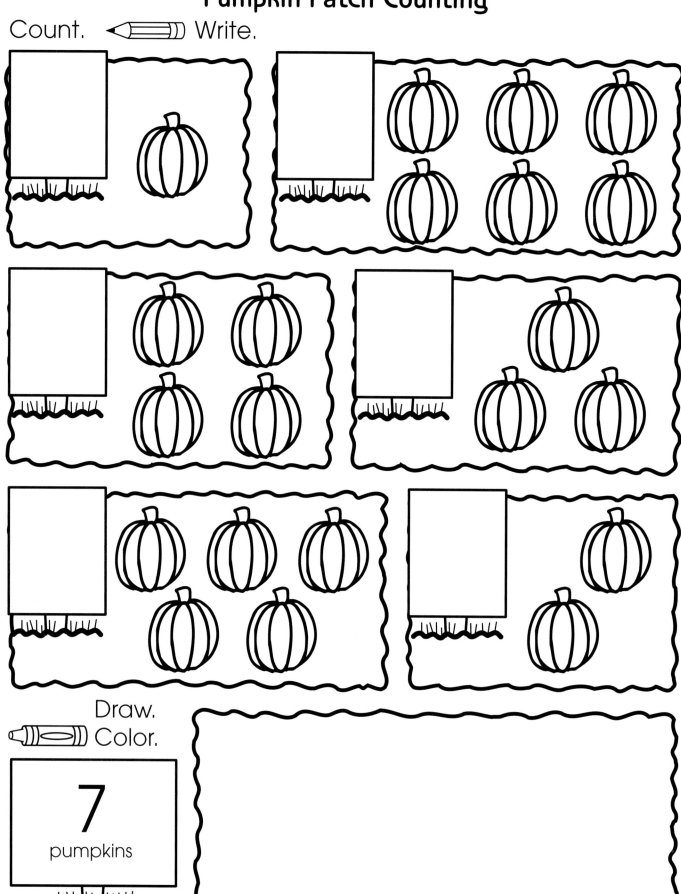 Write.

Draw.
Color.

7
pumpkins

Playing With Pumpkin Seeds

Read.

Count.

 Glue or draw .

Name _____

Pumpkin Patterning

 Glue on pumpkins.

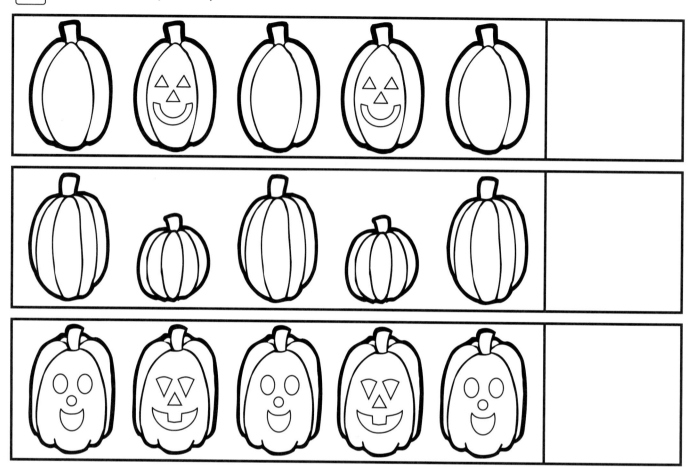

 Glue on pumpkin seeds.

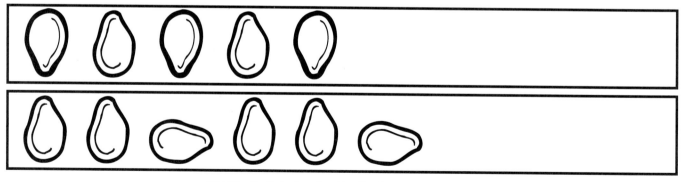

Name _____

Spooky Circles

Trace the ◯ s.

Color the ◯ s.

Name _____

Nosey Triangles

Trace the △s.

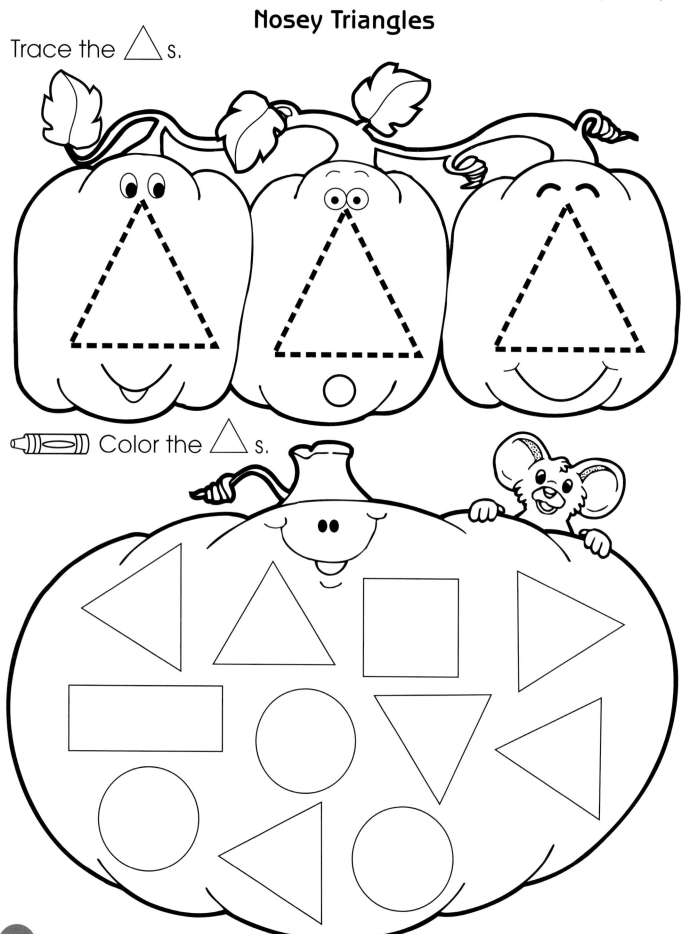

🖍 Color the △s.

Name _____

Silly Squares

Trace the ☐ s.

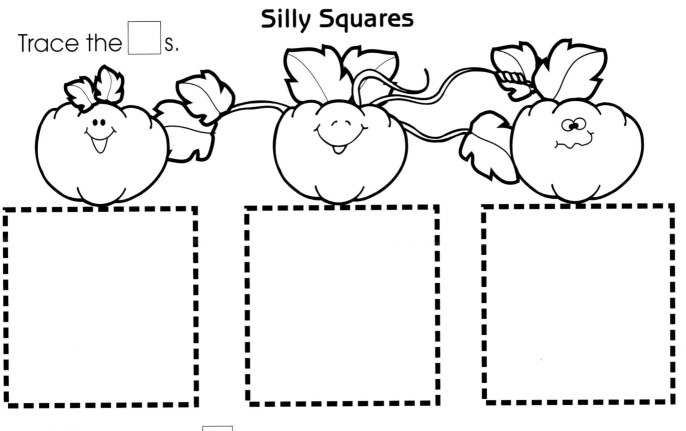

🖍 Color the ☐ s.

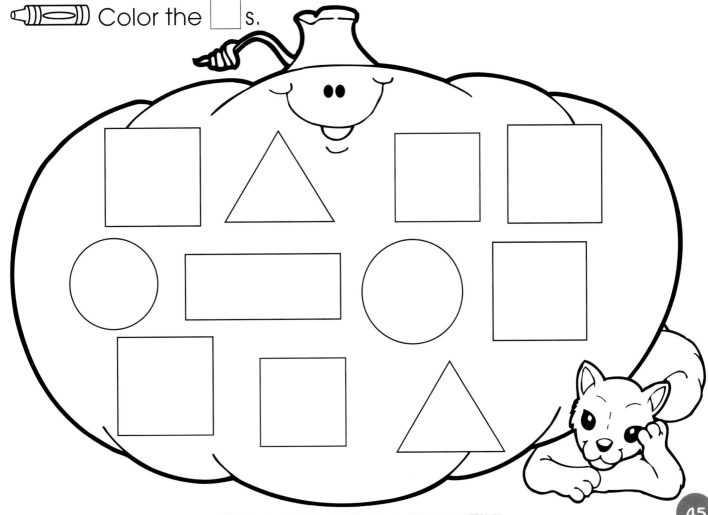

Rectangle Rascals

Trace the ▭s.

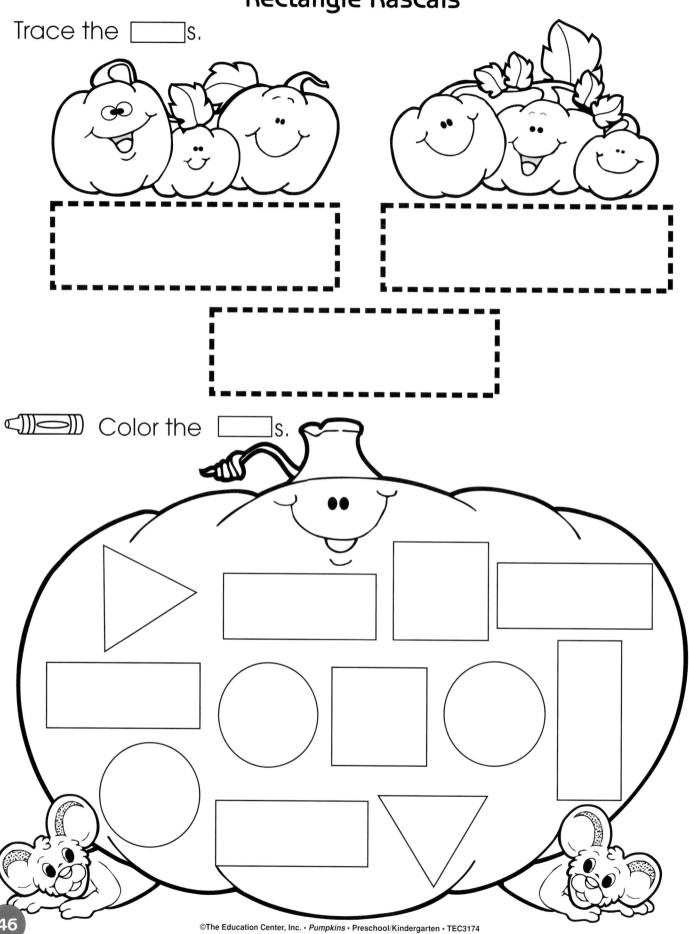

Color the ▭s.

Dear Parent,

Use a real miniature pumpkin to stimulate lots of learning! Do these simple tasks at home with your child and discuss the results with him or her:

1. **Weigh** the pumpkin.
2. **Measure** its height and circumference.
3. Cut open and clean out the pumpkin. **Count** the pumpkin seeds.
4. Find the **big** seeds. Find the **small** seeds. Glue some seeds below.

Have fun!

big seeds

small seeds

Pumpkin Activity Cards

How To Use This Page

Duplicate this page several times on construction paper. Color the pumpkins; cut the cards apart; then laminate them. Use a permanent marker to program the pumpkins with the matching skills of your choice. (For example, program half of the pumpkins with numerals and the other half with corresponding dots.) To do this activity, a child matches each pumpkin card to a corresponding card.

These cards can also be reduced in size and used as game markers for "Clip It!" on page 17.

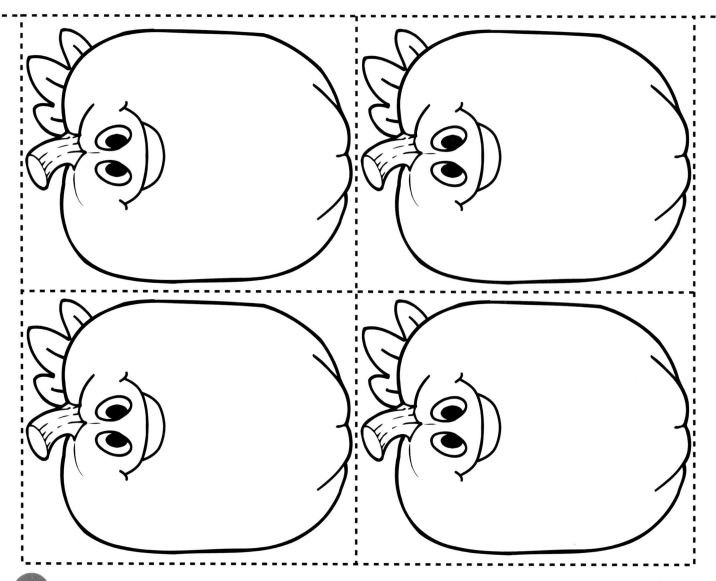